John Lennon

Vanora Leigh

Illustrated by Richard Hook

The Bookwright Press
New York · 1986

Great Lives

William Shakespeare
Queen Elizabeth II
Anne Frank
Martin Luther King, Jr.
Helen Keller
Ferdinand Magellan
Mother Teresa
Louis Braille
John Lennon
John F. Kennedy
Florence Nightingale
Elvis Presley

First published in the
United States in 1986 by
The Bookwright Press
387 Park Avenue South
New York, NY 10016

First published in 1986 by
Wayland (Publishers) Limited
61 Western Road, Hove
East Sussex BN3 1JD, England

ISBN 0–531–18072–7
Library of Congress Catalog Card Number: 85–73676

Phototypeset by Kalligraphics Ltd, Redhill, Surrey
Printed in Italy by G. Canale & C.S.p.A., Turin

Contents

Living legends

The Beatles were almost certainly the greatest pop group Britain has ever produced. Many people would say they were the greatest pop group *any* country has produced! They became legendary figures in their own lifetimes, pursued by the press and idolized by the young.

It has been said that a new musical era began with the Beatles and that they widened the popular appeal of rock music as no other performers had ever done before. In 1964 they challenged American supremacy of the world's pop charts and won, even in the United States itself. Their popularity lasted right through the so-called "swinging sixties," those years when London became the most fashionable

The Beatles at the height of their success.

capital city in the world.

Yet the Beatles themselves changed considerably during the following six years. The four cheeky, boy-next-door types, with distinctive hair-cuts and neat, collarless suits, become four long-haired, often untidy, frequently quarrelsome individuals. Their music changed too, becoming more complex but never losing that essential Beatles' originality and brilliance. Today, the individual Beatles – Paul McCartney, George Harrison, Ringo Starr and John Lennon – remain household names, even though they last appeared together in 1969. Now, with the exception of John, who was murdered in 1980, they all enjoy different, but equally successful, careers.

Of all the Beatles, John Lennon has remained the most controversial. He was a man many have called a genius, who produced some of this century's greatest songs and became a spokesman for an entire generation. Yet he could also puzzle his friends and anger those in authority, by his sometimes outrageous behavior. John was never a conformist, yet beneath the witty, sharp, often hard

exterior, there was a man who had known too much tragedy. Within one ten-year period his mother, his best friend and his manager, all died. His own early death was the greatest tragedy of all.

John performing at one of his last concerts.

Aunt Mimi

On October 9, 1940, John Winston Lennon was born in Liverpool. Britain was at war with Germany and, in a patriotic moment, the baby's mother, Julia, decided to give her son a middle name that belonged to the country's wartime leader, Winston Churchill.

John's father, Freddie, was a ship's waiter who was away from home for most of the war and then vanished from his young son's life. When John's parents' marriage finally ended, his mother married another man who had children of his own and didn't want John.

It would have been a bleak and unhappy childhood for the little boy had it not been for his Aunt Mimi (Julia's sister) and Uncle George. They gave him a home and loved him as if he had been their own child.

When he was four John started school. He soon proved to be a quick learner and was good at reading, writing stories and drawing. As he grew older he also liked sports such as swimming, but because his eyesight was poor

John at four years old, in his first school uniform.

Although John had been very fond of him, his uncle's death did not affect him as much as that of his mother five years later. Julia had kept in touch with her son during his teenage years and the two had become very good friends. Then she was run over by a car not far from John's home. Following her death he became very bitter.

John and Aunt Mimi.

he did not much enjoy playing soccer or other similar ball games.

As a boy, John was regarded by people outside his home, especially teachers, as a nuisance. Yet at home he was well behaved and polite. His Aunt Mimi was strict but always caring and had a great influence on John's early life.

When John was twelve years old his Uncle George died.

Making music

The Quarrymen: Paul is on the left and John in the middle.

In 1956, Aunt Mimi bought John a guitar and with a schoolfriend, Peter Shotton, he formed a skiffle duo. They named themselves the Quarrymen, after their school, Quarry Bank Grammar. Other friends were recruited and the group started playing at youth clubs and entering talent competitions.

At one of these early appearances, the group was seen by another Liverpool youngster, Paul McCartney. Paul was already a good musician and when John heard him he was very impressed. Acknowledged as the Quarrymen's leader, he invited Paul to join them. The two boys got on well and were soon writing their first songs.

It was Paul's turn next to introduce a new name into the group, a boy called George

Although John's world revolved around music, his Aunt Mimi worried about her nephew's education. Despite being very bright, he left Quarry Bank Grammar School in 1957 after failing his "O-levels" (exams). But John was a talented artist and Mimi agreed that he should attend Liverpool Art College.

John worked no harder at college than he had done at school but he did meet two students who became close and important friends in his life. One was a pretty, quiet girl called Cynthia Powell. She tolerated John's frequent outbursts of bad temper and rudeness. For his part, John was protective, a trait which, unfortunately, often developed into jealousy and possessiveness. Soon John and Cynthia were "going steady."

Stuart Sutcliffe was the other student who became John's close friend. He was a gifted artist and dressed in a distinctive fashion. These two off-beat characters liked each other immediately. "Stu" encouraged John with his art and he soon became a member of the Quarrymen group, even though he knew little about music.

Harrison. Although he was only fourteen when he joined John and Paul in 1958, George was already an excellent musician and became lead guitarist.

During the group's early days, several youngsters joined, left and were replaced. But once John, Paul and George were together they formed a musical heart for the Quarrymen.

Birth of the Beatles

Success did not come easily to the Quarrymen. Members of the group had lots of energy and enthusiasm but looked – and sounded – like amateurs. Their musical equipment was poor and they frequently found themselves without a drummer. They had moved away from the skiffle craze in 1959 but had still not found a style of their own.

Instead they imitated popular American singers of the time. Even a change of name, to Johnny and the Moondogs, failed to boost their popularity.

It was Stu Sutcliffe who suggested that the group call themselves the Beetles. John, who liked to pun with words, changed this to the Beatles and then added Silver to the name.

George, Paul and John, with Pete Best in the foreground.

As the Silver Beatles, the group were discovered playing in a Liverpool coffee bar by a pop music promoter called Larry Parnes. He offered the group – who by then had found themselves a temporary drummer – the chance to tour Scotland and the north of England as support group to his singers. This was a depressing experience for the boys but audiences liked them.

After several months playing at local dances, the group had the offer of traveling to Germany to play at a club in Hamburg. Although their drummer had left, they found a new one called Pete Best. Hamburg proved as miserable an experience as touring in Britain had been. The club was small and gloomy and the group was expected to play for long hours.

Yet before returning penniless to Liverpool, the group had made certain changes. They now called themselves the Beatles (dropping the prefix Silver) and had acquired the hairstyle, combed forward into thick bangs, that was to become their trademark. This hairstyle was the idea of a young German designer, Astrid Kirchnerr, who had fallen in love with Stu Sutcliffe.

The Cavern

The Beatles' experience in Hamburg may have been disappointing but their long hours of work on stage had greatly improved their performances. They now looked and sounded professional and had not been back home long before they were seen by an influential Liverpool disc jockey named

Bob Wooler.

It was Bob who managed to get the Beatles a booking at a club where he was working. That club, in a dingy basement in the center of Liverpool, was to become world famous – thanks to the Beatles. It was called the Cavern. In those days there were five Beatles – John, Paul, George, Stu and Pete. John and Paul would stand together playing their guitars and singing, George played his guitar standing to one side, Stu, still a poor musician, played with his back to the audience and Pete, on the drums, attracted the girls!

Despite their previous unhappy trip to Germany, the group returned in 1961 and it was then that Stu decided to leave. He enrolled at art school, married Astrid and died unexpectedly of a brain hemorrhage the following year. John was devastated by the news of his closest friend's death.

It was in 1961, during the Beatles' second trip to Germany, that they made their first recording, including *My Bonnie*, which was released as a single and became very successful in Germany. A few copies arrived in Britain, and the Beatles made sure that Bob Wooler received one. The DJ liked the record and began to play it at the Cavern Club. Soon youngsters began asking for *My Bonnie* in local record stores, one of which was managed by a young man called Brian Epstein. He went to see the group at the club and realized that with a manager to guide them, they had the potential to go right to the top.

The Liver Building in Liverpool, the Beatles' home town and birthplace of the "Mersey Beat."

Taking off

Brian Epstein was a businessman, not a musician but he did have contacts in the music world. Early in 1962 he managed to get the Beatles an audition with Decca Records, but this was not a success. Similarly, they were turned down by other giant recording companies such as Pye, Philips, Columbia and HMV! Groups were thought to be on the way out and the pop charts were dominated by solo performers like Cliff Richard.

Undeterred, Epstein continued to encourage the Beatles and made them improve their image. They started to wear suits instead of jeans and he saw to it that they were always punctual for appointments. In the summer of 1962, his faith in the

George, Paul and John with their manager, Brian Epstein.

John and Cynthia with Ringo and his wife Maureen.

group paid off when George Martin, who ran Parlophone Records, agreed to give them an audition.

Although he liked the Beatles, George Martin did not think that Pete Best was a good enough drummer. The popular Best was fired and Liverpool fans reacted angrily – one even gave George Harrison a black eye. It didn't take long to find a replacement, a young drummer the Beatles had first seen in Hamburg, called Richard Starkey, or Ringo Starr as he became known.

August and September of that year were important months for John. He married his long-time girl friend, Cynthia, in August. Their son, Julian, was born in April the following year.

In September, John and the other members of the group went to the studios of EMI, at Abbey Road, London, to record their first single. The song on side one – *Love Me Do* – was written by John and Paul, with John singing as well as playing the harmonica. By December the record was in the Top Twenty and four young men were about to shoot to super-stardom.

Four individuals

Much of the Beatles' attraction was that they seemed genuinely down-to-earth, all sharing a sense of fun and dislike of the "establishment." These characteristics came across in TV interviews and in their performances. Yet they shared more than a love of music and joking. Their four personalities blended so well together that, according to Paul, they were really four parts of the same person: John was always regarded as the brains of the group!

Three of the four Beatles shared similarly disrupted childhoods. John had been abandoned by his parents and brought up by his aunt. Like John, Paul's mother had died while her son was in his teens and he had been brought up by his father, a salesman and part-time jazz musician. Ringo's father had left home while Ringo was still a small boy. Only George had enjoyed a normal home life; he was the fourth child of a large family of brothers and sisters.

Although they all enjoyed clowning around together, on and off stage, the Beatles had very different temperaments. Despite the group's success, they were four individuals who happened to complement each other perfectly. John was quick-tempered with a sharp mind and tongue while Paul was the charming spokesman for the group. Girls thought him "sweet," a word they would never have used to describe John! Paul worked hard, liked an audience and was ambitious; John often wrote only for his own amusement and could be lazy.

The Lennon/McCartney song-writing partnership meant that the other two Beatles, George and Ringo, did not attract as much personal publicity as John and Paul. George, the youngest Beatle, always remained the least talkative member of the group, and gained a reputation for being "serious." Ringo, the oldest Beatle, who had replaced Pete Best as drummer, was a relaxed, uncomplicated person, liked by everybody and as well known for his large nose and the rings on his fingers as he was for his drumming!

Beatlemania

In 1963 the Beatles took the world by storm. The year began with an appearance on a successful TV show, where they performed their latest single, *Please, Please Me*. Yet who could have predicted that by the year's end, the "Fab Four" would have been praised by a well-known music critic, appeared before royalty and been described as, "the biggest thing ever in pop music?"

The Beatles worked very hard throughout the year. Although on the brink of becoming the most famous pop group ever, they certainly could not take life easy. They toured as the support group for famous singing stars, but their overwhelming popularity put them at the top of the bill half-way through one tour.

Hit records were released in a constant stream, with songs written by John and Paul. The two had such an astounding output that they already had over a hundred compositions to their names. Their first LP *Please, Please Me* soared to the top of the British charts in May, giving

Beatles' fans line up for three days and nights for tickets to a concert.

way, six months later, to their second, *With the Beatles*.

Not only did the Beatles make records – they broke them, too! Their third single, *From Me To You*, was their first number one. All of their next ten singles also went to number one. *She Loves You*, released in August, was the first of five Beatles singles to sell over a million copies, and stayed on the British charts for thirty-one weeks.

Now, wherever the Beatles performed, there were scenes of hysteria, with screaming, weeping girls almost drowning the music, and the word Beatlemania was invented.

By the end of the year, the Beatles had become a legend.

Over 15 million people in Britain watched them on a TV performance. Their second album was praised by *The Times* of London and they appeared before royalty at the Royal Variety Performance. Here John Lennon joked "Would those in the cheap seats clap their hands? The rest of you can rattle your jewelery!"

The four Beatles and Brian Epstein meet Princess Margaret.

The Beatles in America

The next goal for the Beatles was the United States. In January 1964 their single *I Want to Hold Your Hand* topped the U.S. charts. The following month the Beatles themselves went to the United States. They received an ecstatic welcome from their fans, appeared on a popular TV show and filled Carnegie Hall in New York City.

In 1964 the Beatles made their first movie, *A Hard Day's Night*, which was very successful. Still their records continued to dominate the charts on both sides of the Atlantic, in Europe, Australia and in New Zealand. Tours all over the world were arranged, including a return visit to America, where even Frank Sinatra tried to get tickets to a Beatles concert – and failed!

The success of the Beatles' first movie ensured that there were offers to make more. The follow-up to *A Hard Day's Night* was *Help!*, which proved just as popular. The movie had a royal première. Besides royalty, the

On tour in the United States.

A scene from the movie Help!

Beatles numbered politicans among their fans, including British Prime Minister Harold Wilson, at whose instigation the Beatles were awarded MBEs (Members of the Order of the British Empire) in 1965.

American fans continued to demand personal appearances by the group. Later in 1965, they returned to the United States and gave concerts before huge audiences. They could do no wrong in the country until Americans heard about a remark that John had made to a newspaper reporter. He was reported to have said that the Beatles were now, in his opinion, more popular than Jesus. Some states threatened to ban the Beatles and John had to apologize.

It was already becoming clear that the Beatles were slowly drifting apart, as each developed separate interests. Yet they continued to produce best-selling records together in 1966 and 1967. Some of their most popular songs were made at this time, including their memorable LP, *Sgt. Pepper's Lonely Hearts Club Band.*

Everything the Beatles touched still turned to gold, but the frenzy of Beatlemania belonged to the early and mid-sixties, not the later years.

Eastern influence

The Beatles were very honest about their experiments with drugs. So it came as a surprise when, in 1967, they told the press that they had given up all drug taking.

The reason was a meeting they had had with an eastern guru, Maharishi Mahesh Yogi, who was given the nickname the "Giggling Guru." He offered the Beatles transcendental meditation, rather than drugs, as a means of finding peace and relaxation. They went to hear him lecture, in Wales, but on the second day were shocked by the news that their manager, Brian Epstein, had died from a drugs overdose in his London apartment.

In the following year the group decided to visit the Maharishi in India. This much publicized visit was planned to last three months but for Ringo it ended after ten days, when he returned, homesick and ill. Paul returned nine weeks later and John and George soon followed. They were all disenchanted with the Guru.

Yoko

Everyone was amazed when John fell in love with Yoko Ono, a Japanese woman several years older than himself and certainly not the little girl "groupie" type so popular in the sixties. She was an intelligent, strong-minded woman, and a talented artist.

John first met Yoko at an art gallery in London in 1966. They were immediately attracted and began writing to each other regularly. Their relationship grew deeper and in 1968, John and Cynthia's marriage ended in divorce. Yoko went everywhere with John, even being present when the Beatles made a record album, which was seen as an intrusion by the others.

Soon afterward John and Yoko made a record together, which caused newspaper headlines all over the world. On the cover was a photograph of John and Yoko, naked and hand-in-hand. They were married in 1969 and continued to shock by spending a seven-day peace vigil in bed in an Amsterdam hotel, to which they invited the press.

Going their separate ways

The break-up of the world's most famous pop group happened gradually. It was only natural that four talented young men would also want to pursue their own individual interests outside the Beatles. John was the first to make a name for himself. In 1964 his first book, containing witty drawings and writings, called *John Lennon – In His Own Write*, was published. The following year, another book, *A Spaniard in the Works*, appeared. Both were very successful.

In 1966 John made his debut as a straight actor in the movie *How I Won The War*, while Paul was busy writing the music for another movie. Ringo was enjoying family life and George was involved with Indian music. But 1967, the year of one of the Beatles' greatest hits, *All You Need Is Love*, had marked the real beginning of the end of the group, with the death of their manager, Brian Epstein.

John plays a straight role in the movie How I Won the War.

Although Brian's brother Clive became their new manager, the Beatles now began to make more decisions on their own, often with disastrous results. They made a movie, *Magical Mystery Tour*, which was poorly received, and at the end of 1967 they started their own company, Apple. This proved to be a sour Apple with only the record label being a success. The

The Beatles promoting their famous peace record, All You Need is Love.

The Apple Boutique in Baker Street, London.

famous Apple boutique in London lasted just seven months.

Yet their records were still widely acclaimed: *The White Album* released in 1968, *Yellow Submarine* the following year and *Abbey Road*, also in 1969. Their last public appearance together was in January 1969, when they were filmed singing *Let It Be* on the roof of the Apple building in London. At the end of 1970, after arguments over finance and management, the group officially split when Paul McCartney began legal proceedings to end the Beatles partnership. It was left to John to sum up the glorious Beatle years when he commented: "Everyone had a good time."

"Give peace a chance"

As the split which was dividing the Beatles widened, John's way of life was changing rapidly. World peace was the subject that preoccupied him and his new wife, Yoko Ono. In 1969, the year in which the couple married, John composed his famous song, *Give Peace A Chance* and handed back his MBE in protest at British involvement in wars in Vietnam and Nigeria. His records, either solo performances or with Yoko and the Plastic Ono Band, were now based on his own personal thoughts and the state of the world. Away from the Beatles John became more serious and produced material that was not always a commercial success.

Until the summer of 1971, John and Yoko lived in England, but they found life increasingly boring and moved to New York. John found the city so exciting that he told a reporter: "I should

have been born in New York."

He soon became involved with political protest groups, which didn't please the United States government. President Richard Nixon became so worried about John's activities that his supporters tried to get John removed from the United States.

In 1973 John and Yoko's marriage temporarily broke up. John went to Los Angeles where he was often seen drinking with other musicians. Fortunately, he met Yoko again after a concert in New York the following year. The couple mended their broken relationship and in 1975, Yoko gave birth to John's second son, Sean.

For the next four years, John became a recluse, looking after Sean and rarely moving outside the building in New York where he and Yoko had an apartment. The couple had few friends, preferring each other's company and that of their son. On the rare occasions when John did go out, he would be asked when the Beatles would get back together again. To him, it seemed pointless to answer because he knew they never would.

Relaxing at his home.

A new beginning is shattered

Recording with Yoko.

found true contentment with his wife and son. His fans, who had almost given up hope of ever seeing him in the spotlight again, welcomed him back, but they were surprised by his cheerful image. Even his new songs had happy lyrics and these disappointed some people who expected – and enjoyed – the anger, wit, and flair for the off-beat that had become the old John Lennon trademarks.

John Lennon met his death

It was 1980, the start of a new decade, when John Lennon decided to come out of his self-imposed period of musical inactivity and make records again. One of the main reasons was that his small son Sean was almost five and would soon be starting school, giving John plenty of free time. Working with Yoko, he made an LP called *Double Fantasy*.

John was forty in 1980 and seemed to be enjoying life. After his turbulent childhood and the almost unreal years as a Beatle, it looked as if he had finally

outside his home in New York. On the afternoon of December 8, 1980, he signed an autograph for Mark David Chapman. Five hours later, as John was going into his apartment block, Chapman called his name and then shot him several times. John died within minutes in the back of a police car rushing him to hospital.

Millions of fans around the world mourned John's tragic death. Radio and TV stations in many countries played Lennon records, especially *Give Peace A Chance* and *Imagine*, a song that John had written and recorded in 1971, shortly before leaving England to live in New York. Thousands of weeping fans kept vigil outside the apartment block, bringing flowers and lighted candles.

John's killer was tried and sent to an institution. Today, few remember him but the name of the man he murdered is as famous now as on the day he died. As Paul McCartney said in a final tribute: "John was a great man who'll be remembered for his unique contributions to art, music and world peace."

Important dates

1940 John's birth in Liverpool, England (October 9).
1946 His father leaves home.
1956 While still at school, John forms his first group, the Quarrymen.
1957 John meets Paul McCartney. Joins Liverpool College of Art.
1958 John's mother, Julia, is killed in a car crash.
      John meets George Harrison.
1960 Calling themselves the Beatles, the group go to Germany.
1961 The Beatles are seen by Brian Epstein at The Cavern.
1962 Stuart Sutcliffe dies.
      The Beatles sign a record contract with EMI.
      Ringo Starr joins the group.
      John marries Cynthia Powell.
1963 John and Cythia's son Julian is born.
      Royal Variety Show appearance for the Beatles.
1964 The Beatles are a huge success in the United States.
      John's first book, *In His Own Write*, is published.
      The Beatles make their first movie *A Hard Day's Night*.
1965 The four Beatles are awarded MBEs.
      John's second book, *A Spaniard in the Works*, is published.
      The Beatles appear before 15,600 fans at Shea Stadium, New York.

1966 The last Beatles concert. John meets Yoko Ono.
1967 The Maharishi enters the Beatles' lives.
      Brian Epstein is found dead.
      John stars in the movie *How I Won the War*.
      Apple company formed.
1968 Cynthia Lennon divorces John.
1969 Last public appearance by the Beatles.
      John marries Yoko Ono.
1971 John and Yoko go to live in New York.
1973 John and Yoko separate.
1974 John and Yoko are reunited.
1975 Their son, Sean, is born.
1980 John appears in public again. He is shot dead in New York (December 8).

Picture credits

Glossary

Conformist   Someone who always does what other people do.

Controversial   Causing argument or debate.

Controversy   A dispute, argument or discussion.

Debut   The first public appearance in a particular role – in this case as a serious actor.

Duo   A pair of musical performers.

Era   A period of time that is considered as having a distinctive character.

Guru   An eastern religious teacher.

Hysteria   A frenzied emotional state.

Intrusion   An unwelcome visit.

Legendary   Very famous.

MBE (Member of the British Empire)   A British award for outstanding achievement, presented by the Queen.

Off-beat   Unusual and unconventional.

Patriotic   Inspired by love of one's country.

Pun   A play on words that have the same sound but different meanings.

Recluse   A person who lives a quiet life away from the company of others.

Skiffle   A style of British popular music of the 1950s, played chiefly on guitars and percussion instruments.

Supremacy   The position of being above all others.

Transcendental meditation   A technique, based on Hindu traditions, for relaxing and refreshing the mind and body.

The Establishment   The group in a society that acts in the accepted tradition and holds accepted opinions, usually people in authority within the society.

Vigil   A watch during which people may pray or mourn, often at a shrine.

Books to read

Domnitz, Linda D. *John Lennon Conversations*. Farmingdale, NY: Coleman Publishing, 1984.

Lennon, John. *In His Own Write & A Spaniard in the Works*. New York: New American Library, 1981.

John Lennon, et al. *The Last Lennon Tapes*. New York: Dell, 1983.

McCabe, Peter. *John Lennon: The Lost Tapes*. New York: Bantam, 1984.

Ono, Yoko. *The Summer of Nineteen Eighty*. New York: Putnam Publishing Group, 1983.

Index